Fleeting Love

Fleeting Love

For all those who have
ever felt Left Out,
Unloved or Unwanted

KHUSHI SUNDERKA

LAUNCHPAD

An imprint of
Srishti Publishers & Distributors

Srishti Publishers & Distributors
A unit of AJR Publishing LLP
212A, Peacock Lane
Shahpur Jat, New Delhi – 110 049
editorial@srishtipublishers.com

First published by Launchpad,
an imprint of Srishti Publishers & Distributors in 2026

10 9 8 7 6 5 4 3 2 1

For all those who have ever felt
left out, unloved or unwanted

Gar panno par dard byaan karne se dard beh jaate hai
to mere marhum ban gaye hai siyaahii…

Pain is the foundation of this book.
I thank the pain that gave me the strength to bare my soul and show you the deepest corner of my heart I once hid…

For all those who suffered in silence,

for all those who endure pain inside,

for all those who are battling with their inner demons,

for all those whose wounds have never been touched by anyone with love,

for all those whose pain was ignored,

for those who defeated the pain and bloomed like a beautiful flower,

and lastly,

for those who know how to love themselves before loving someone else.

The motive of this book is not to give you the so called "GYAAN" or stereotyped lessons, but to expose the raw emotions buried within you.

Those unspoken feelings you've hidden away? This book speaks to them.

Simplicity often holds the deepest truths. Words, I believe, have the power to heal, and perhaps these words will find a way to heal your wounds, to help you rediscover the sunlight you've been searching for.

Maybe, just maybe, you'll find yourself in one of these pages.

Through this book, I want you to know that we are all sailors in the same boat; it's just that our ways of expressing our feelings are different.

Just a reminder: YOU ARE NOT ALONE.

Every dark night is followed by a sunrise; let this book be that light for you.

Whether you're nursing a broken heart, rediscovering yourself, or simply reflecting on the love you've given and received, this book will speak to you.

Take a chance. Let this book remind you of your strength, beauty, and your heart's endless capacity to heal and love again.

You are not alone, and you are enough.

Maybe someday
you'll read the poems
I wrote about you.

Loving Intensely

Love isn't just a feeling...

It's a selfless act of giving, of placing another's happiness above your own.

You liked me,
and I thought you loved me.
I started loving you,
even though I didn't want to fall.
I'm trapped now.

With each passing moment,
I find myself getting more
and more enmeshed with you.
I had no idea,
there would be no option of UNDO,
only REDO.

I put my heart on the plate of those I love,
to the extent that it breaks me.
But alas, it was not enough.
They walked over, saying,
"We didn't ask you to."

Is it my fault to love others more than myself?
It hits me like a bullet.
I had a hard way learning…
Someone's inability to see my goodness
or appreciate who I am,
doesn't make me UNLOVED.

What is home for you?

For some,
Home is not just concrete and walls,
It is the person
who is close to their soul.

Our home is where our true love belongs,
where our heart lies.

I like black coffee,
In it, I taste the bitterness…
You left in me.

It makes me weep,
I'll never stop consuming it.

I'd rather have you
in your darkest moments than not at all.
That's how I love you.
And even though I hate black coffee,
I'm still falling in love even more,
as it reminds me of you.

I refuse
to allow you
to fill the voids in my being.

To be whole is what I seek.
Together,
We set the city on fire.

I need someone
who listens to my silent screams,
someone who understands my words
when I'm silent.

I shall perish,
for I am an unloved person
Still searching for
unconditional love.

I wanted to build a life with you,
not mould me into yours.

I am not sure.
Is what I am experiencing love?

I feel empty
when you are not around.
What particular emotion am I experiencing?

I felt unworthy of you
when we were together.
I feel like there's not enough of me
without you.

I often question
If it was a mistake
to love you so deeply.

while continuing to bear
such extreme pain in the process.
But I know that if I hadn't
I never would have discovered
what love truly is.

I don’t regret loving you,
I believe there’s beauty in it,
even if you are not loved back.

You left my life,
leaving me behind.
But you remained in my poetry
and will always remain in my words.

Beauty cannot be defined by faces…
It's defined by heart.

I must part from you,
like smoke from a cigarette.
You consume me,
From inside out.
Just like a cigarette
hollowing out a person from within.

I know you harm me.
I'm still devouring you,
much like people still consume cigarettes
despite seeing the warning on them.
Like a cigarette,
you are a slow poison to me.

Just like a doomed crush…
One-sided love has the ability to exist,
even when it isn't visible.

Even though you cannot claim
it as your own.

He was effortlessly in love with me.
He helped me
realise how whole I am
in my own eyes.

We yearn to be loved effortlessly,
and we seek to love effortlessly.

I have a story to tell.
Some have love,
Some have tears,
Some have heartbreaks,
Some have shattered hopes.
Perhaps the most flawless stories
have some flaws too.

I heard somewhere,
"Zindagi itni khubsurat kyun hoti hai?"
"Kyunki wo khatam hoti hai."

Maybe that could be a reason
of loving you more…
You aren't mine anymore.

We are constantly in love
with what we do not have.

I love you far enough
that you've never truly died to me.

Do you honestly believe
love can be so profound
that you can lock your soul
in someone's corpse?
Or are stories like these limited to fiction?

His absence makes me feel
more detached from myself.
My existence was
eternally bound to his.

Deep down,
we are all poets,
we simply must allow it to happen.

My presence means nothing to you
If it doesn't change your life.

There are a few poems I've written,
which aren't for everyone.
But for a few people.

That portion of you
and your feelings are reserved
for certain people.

Sometimes, just one person.

You prefer black and white,
I am a person of grey.

I know you like the moon,
But the magic happens for me
in the stars.
I know we have completely different personalities,
but can we just pretend
To fall in love…
With opposite choices?

You are a poem,
I find a different meaning
no matter how many times
I read it.

You are the poem
I have always wanted to read.

You are the poem in my diary that
I don't want anyone else to read.

What is the perfect definition of insanity?

Is it repeating the same thing
over and over
and hoping for different results?

Love is defined precisely.

Getting Hurt

If it fails to bring pain, what sort of love is that?

Is this the price of loving you
more than loving myself?

I'm shrinking,
I'm floating,
I'm drowning.
So what?

This is the cost of loving you harder.

I can shrink
If you are with me.
I can break
my heart for you…
while it mends yours.

I know
holding you
will only hurt me.

It is hurting me.
Tearing me apart.

I want to let it go.
I'm still holding on.

It's tragic.
I neither want to hold,
nor let you go.

We are so comfortable with pain that
when happiness knocks on the door,
it seems unreal.
You become so used to bearing pain
that you forget to feel happiness.
Maybe you feel that
this happiness is a deception
that will not stay with you for long,
sadness is bound to come.

It hurts
when someone constantly gives you pain,
yet you still choose to stay
until it swallows you.

Maybe
you live in this illusion
that suffering will eventually disappear,
or that it will not hurt you as much.

The happiest of faces,
broken to the core
and left with no energy to carry on.
That's how depression is.

The most dangerous thing?
When your biggest excitement
and your biggest disappointment
come from the same person.

Despite our enough capacity of love,
we nevertheless choose to be poisonous.

I'm not the appetizer you crave occasionally at parties,
I'm the food you need to survive.

Don't come to me expecting something fleeting
or trying to turn me into a holiday destination.

I'm Home.
Not a Holiday Destination.

The poetry breaks me into millions of pieces.
I still choose to write,
as you are a part of my words.
And I still choose to break
Until my ink bleeds with
the pain of losing you.

I read a quote somewhere,
"If it doesn't hurt,
it isn't love."

And every time he hurt me,
I thought he was loving me.
I thought this was how,
love was supposed to be.

If I could,
I would take you on an inspection of my overthinking
to show how you destroyed me.

I would take you on an excursion
and drive you to witness it over and over
If I could.

The worst thing about loving someone?
You start expecting the same amount of love...
You poured into them.

It takes away your ability
to fall in love again.

There are moments when
sorrow brings serenity,
and moments when
happiness brings vanity.

When you don't talk about
what's upsetting you...
A relationship can never be fixed
or restored.

Emotions cannot be eliminated
by holding them inside.
They do not go away easily
when bottled up.

Bottling up your emotions causes
irreparable animosity.
It damages the relationship.

Avoid being with someone
whose life is a blur.
Showing you
the things they wish they had done
but didn't.

Outside my mess,
it is tough to love me.

No one can guess,
what's hidden inside.

Problems find my address
before anyone else can reach me.

Tears fall down my cheeks
before I say anything.

I'm a complete mess.

My numbness screams
through my silence.

Will you accept me with all my flaws?
Will you still love me?

To keep the flames blazing,
to keep moving and wanting,
I traded my heart one more time
with each step I took.
My suffering served as my fuel.

In his deep breaths,
the heart sensed
more than the words
he never spoke.

It felt as though
he was ablaze beneath
a layer of snow.

Those who impose pain on others
often carry it inside.

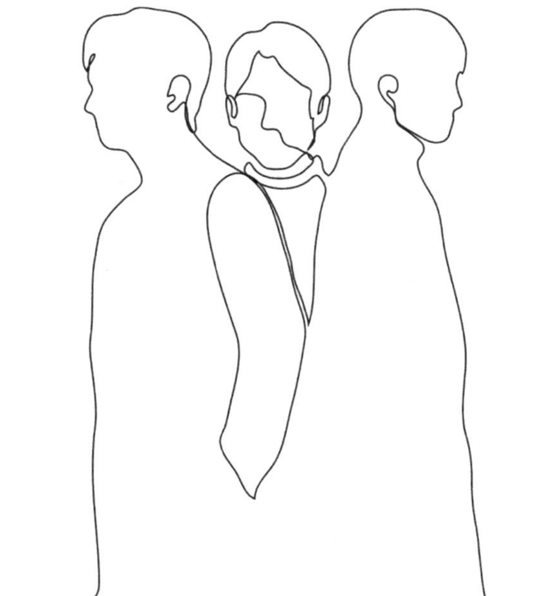

It's miserable
how we continue to look
for hope from the same person
who abandoned us.

Few people will make you feel hopeful
but ultimately leave you feeling empty.
Keep moving away from them
to prevent your heart from breaking.
Control your emotions
before they shatter you.

The worst state for a person's heart?
Wanting to cling on
and let go of at the same time.

Sometimes,
even the prettiest things on the surface
might serve as a facade
for the chaos within.

When your heart is full of love
for someone who constantly
makes you feel unworthy of love,
it is often the heaviest thing
You have to carry.

When someone breaks your heart,
you feel like breaking everything.
Perhaps
this's why smash rooms
have become so popular.

It's never the person leaving
who is sad,
always the one left behind.

Instead of discarding or hiding broken things,
you should find beauty in their brokenness
and transform them into something extraordinary.

Every broken part reveals a story about
how much he has destroyed himself
by embracing someone else.

How could that one person be the reason
for all your sufferings and solace?

No matter how much you try
to fill the glass of your happiness with love,
there are people who try to break
you in every possible manner.
Make you empty and hollow inside.

Perhaps your enthusiasm chokes them.

The person who used to make me happy
is now a part of my sufferings.

You are the ocean
who continually appears in my eyes
in the form of tears.

Old Wounds

The more intense the love, the deeper the wound it causes

People say,
love is a bird that gives
you wings to fly.

Love is a bird that can
take you to new heights.

But sometimes
love feels like a nylon thread…

It rips your heart apart and bleeds
all over the floor,
leaving it deep red.

Happiness comes from making memories
with the people who make you feel at home,
not from the places you've been to.

In my heart,
every tiny detail of you and
your memories are fresh like orchids.
I wish to let them go,
I wish to let go…
But I hold on to them.
That's the worst state
one's heart can be in.

By getting hurt,
we become used to it.
we consider this pain our home,
where we belong.

You are no longer the same as before.
The fragrance gets lost somewhere,
and some voids are not meant to be filled.

When someone is dripping artificial sugar syrup,
proceed with caution.
Perhaps they are looking for your real honey.

You don't get affected
by your old wounds.

It feels like a lie
when people care
because, in reality,
nobody does.

Everybody lies.

My silence becomes the loudest,
when I lock my heart tight.

Even silence can make the loudest noise,
when I bottle up my emotions.

I always thought keeping things inside
was the best way to move on.

I was building a wall within myself.
Living in a cocoon.

Didn't realize
My silence became too loud to handle.

How tragic!
I loved you so deeply
And you chose "YOU" over "US".

Now,
when you choose to live with me,
my love for you is no longer the same.

My love for you has been buried
deep in a tomb,
it will never be retrieved.

People never come
when they are wanted.

They come when
they are neither wanted nor needed.
Don't be late to come back.

Every time I think of you,
there is a spot
in my heart that bleeds.

You only harmed me once,
since I was the one who
kept repeating the same scenario
over and over in my mind,
making it worse every time.

I wrote so many letters
that I never gave to you.

Never had the courage to send them.

Maybe I thought
you would not understand.

Letters remained confined to the pages,
Never reached you.

I still write letters,
but only to release my heart from the pain.
Writing is the only way of healing my wounds,
I found solace in it.

I saw you walk into the garden of my heart,
bring spring into my life.
I saw you,
Saw the season of spring
turned into autumn fall.

You left me behind,
But you continue to exist
Inside me
A void in my soul.

When I planted flowers in my broken vase,
I found
damaged things can also sprout life.
Damaged yet beautiful.

She writes poetry
the way she used to heal his wounds.

My wounded heart seeks
solace in loneliness.

I feel like these streets are extremely
possessive over me,
choking me to the core
every time I visit this city.

Bottling up emotions is like storing a wave.
You have no idea to what extent this can
ruin your life.
You'll not even realize when
this wave will destroy your life
and go away.
Just one wave is enough to shatter everything.

You should let go
of memories that only cause you pain.

I walled myself off from the world
Nothing would hurt me.

But it also blocked happiness
from reaching me.

Sometimes,
the happiest memories hurt you the most.

There are some questions in life
that will never truly have answers,
they will always remain unanswered.

Dying Love

Everything comes with an expiry date

It happened,
and it still hurts.
I tried to mend the broken pieces,
But I don't know how to mend them.
I talk,
I talk a lot,
but it was never in front of you,
It was never with you.
It was always in my head,
in my mind,
which slowly broke my heart
and soul.
My conversations were always
within me,
not between us.

You left me with an empty space
hoping to be filled
with you and your love,
But you don't want to fill it.

I think you like to keep
things unfilled and empty.

Maybe your heart is already overflowing
with the love of someone else.

You used to be the first person in my mind,
Maybe it was the same for you.
The only difference was that
I was never a part of your thoughts.
In my thoughts, it was always you,
and in yours,
it was only you.

People who claim to love me
no longer understand my silence.
They expect me to smile.
I wish I could talk about myself,
but I'm afraid
no one will listen.

Maybe it was my fault to expect
real love in this fake world.

You are just another emptiness in my heart,
waiting to be filled.
You are that pause in my life.

You were so far away that
I didn't even realize you were there.

Knowing that I am your beautiful regret
must burn me inside.

Every time I push you away,
there's a slight hope in my heart
that you will come back.
But that is my false expectation
that drowns me.

You are still clinging to things
that have already passed because
you cannot bear to lose them.

You cannot force someone
to be in love with you.

Holding on is simply harming yourself.

Is it possible to be in love and still
search for someone else's company?

It's bizarre
how we let others
disrespect us
in the name of love.

And one day,
he disappeared from my life
just like the colours faded away
from my painting.

Even broken things can be mended.
Unfortunately, rather than mending
what is damaged,
we are constantly searching for new ones.

Fake smiles,
Grief-stricken faces,
slowly disappearing emotions,
a sensation of deception and
numbness to touch.
Fading old love,
ignoring the existence at home,
this is not love,
it doesn't resonate anymore.

The delusion of
"I'll be with you forever"
has destroyed billions of hopes and dreams.

They said,
"Time will heal everything,
it will change your emotions".

I said,
"Perhaps,
it will merely camouflage the fractured bits
that have nothing left to seal."

He said sorry.
He apologised.
He called me.

He wrote long, drawn-out notes
expressing how much he missed me
and tried to make up for the moments he lost.

He did everything in his power to make amends.
But there are certain things
You cannot UNDO
only REDO.

The love we had is long gone for me.
The damage has already been done.
Will I recover from this wound?
Can you make me whole again?

We are just two strangers who
know each other better than
our own people.

Define love and regret in a single word
YOU

Losing Me

When you try to gain approval from others, you forfeit your own approval. In chasing someone else's love, you might lose the most important love of all… your love for yourself.

Your absence has caused me such excruciating pain
that I find myself having a hard time staying whole.

You left me far away and went
in quest of yourself,
taking my identity with you.
Now, I'm searching for my own existence.

The feeling of being a stranger to myself
made me realise
how hollow I am.

Don't lose yourself in
the process of getting others.

Like the canvas,
there are some gaps that are unfillable.
Some spaces in my heart are intended
to be empty,
no matter how hard I try.

My story is carried by my words,
which reveal my pain on the pages.

I was in the process of loving you
and slowly started losing myself.

Don't invest your time in temporary stuff,
be it people or sentiments.

Once you walked away,
a sense of emptiness began
to consume you.
With someone you were
never together
to begin with,
How do you ask for pardon?

The darkness that dwells within me
constantly finds beauty in catastrophe.
What should I do with my wicked being?

In our desire to be everything
in someone else's life,
we end up being nothing
in our own.

We are losing ourselves in
our longing to have someone else.

The only difference between you and me was
that you were my entire being,
while I was nothing to you.

The world began to recognize my brokenness,
and that's when I realized
how shattered I was.

Another form of salvation is
learning to live with your sorrow
and overcome it every minute.

I searched for that home
where I truly belonged
for years and years,
waiting for this.

I am sick of giving myself to others
who abandon me at my lowest,
I hardly feel bad about
putting myself first.

You gradually begin to lose your own existence
in the face of becoming someone else.

Don't let your light fade
while becoming someone else's shadow.

Don't make your life
a photocopy of someone else's.

Those who make you feel bad
about yourself are often
the ones you love the most.

There is never enough love from me
to make up for the burden that
my presence in people's lives
throws on them.

I could never find someone else
to fill the void
you left in my heart,
that's how you and I
were inseparable.

Why can't we love ourselves
as much as we want to be
loved by others?

Finding Me

Never sacrifice who you are in an attempt to please others.

All you need is to
cut off those
who never valued your love.

Preserve your love for someone
who fills your heart with theirs.

Without knowing the darkness,
you can't find the light within you.
Accepting yourself,
both the good and bad,
is the key to self-discovery.
Become a better version of yourself.

That's how life is:
everyone is self-centred.
They approach you only for
their own interests.

We always seek validation from others,
but have you ever asked yourself
if you truly need approval
from others to make you happy?

Don't let anyone's presence
determine your happiness,
only your own presence can do that.
Be present for yourself,
your presence matters the most.

As time went by,
with each passing day,
I didn't even realize
how I fell in love with
my own company.

Losing you was part of finding myself.

I am a poet.
I release my deepest pain
in the form of poetry.
I find peace in poetry,
I find solace in poetry.
I write about heartbreak
and try to mend many hearts
through my words.

I am giving life to every verse I write
in the form of words.

Accepting your flaws entails
letting them be
without being concerned
about making them perfect.
You give up on the core
of who you are and what makes you
beautiful.
If you let them be in a rebellious way
or make drastic changes in your life.

In her quest to fulfil her highest purpose,
she endured many crushed dreams.

As I was about to go under,
I found an apartment
made of ink and paper below.
It appeared tiny and insignificant,
yet it was a world unto itself.
It helped me to heal,
writing helped me to heal.

Placing recollections beneath my coverlet,
concealing them from the public eye
and combining them into verbatim poetry,
is what she referred to as poetry that
never died.

The wonderful thing about poetry is that
once you start reading it,
you'll always want to read it again,
drawn in by the spaces between the lines.

Do you still need someone
to make you happy,
or can you find happiness
within yourself?

There are times when
I look at myself and feel
that I am no longer the same
cheerful person I used to be.
Maybe now I am mature enough
to deal with things in my own way.

I used to think
my love for you would
always remain unchanged and rigid,
no matter what
even if the world didn't stay
the same.
But now, I feel
my love for you is no
longer the same as it once was.

I was in love with you,
yet you made me feel unworthy.
But now, I realize
I am worthy enough to
let go of those
who are not worthy of me or
who cannot afford my worthiness.

I am not afraid of thunder,
I am a storm inside.

Don't let anyone or anything
overshadow your efforts.

What is your home?

It is the place where
at the slightest inconvenience,
your heart longs to return
the place that makes you feel
comfortable and like you truly belong.
Sometimes,
you may find this home
in the arms of a person.

Gone are the days when
I used to forward him poems
from Google.
Since I started writing,
nothing has resonated with me
except my words and feelings.

To myself:
Thank you for being there
whenever I needed you the most.

There will be days when
you'll appear to be the worst
character in everyone's story.
There will be days when
you feel like disappearing from
everyone's life.
Give yourself some time to reflect
and let everything sink in.
Just remember,
you need yourself more,
you are enough for yourself.
Love yourself.

Gone are the days when
I used to suffer in order to
bring smiles to others' faces.
Now is the time to update my version
who finds bliss within oneself.

Sometimes, I feel that today
I have become what I always wanted to be,
but still, I am not happy.
My life has changed.
A life that was once filled with storms.
And at that time,
the only thing I wanted was
for it to just end.
Now, the storm is over.
Then why am I not at peace?
Maybe I thought I would survive
that storm.
Now, I'm proud of the way I survived.
I just want to be proud of the person
I have become.
But why am I not at peace?
There is a feeling of emptiness-
an unfilled void.
Why has life changed so quickly?
Why has it come to a stop for so long?
Why have there been fewer people?
Why are people disappearing from life?
And why do I find myself changing?
I've reformed myself.

The Healing Journey

Your healing journey begins when you learn to love yourself. Healing is not about moving on; it's about rediscovering joy, learning to love yourself unconditionally, and finding beauty in the cracks.

Not every crack in your heart
shatters you,
some cracks come to make you shine.

Writing gives me strength.
It empowers me even more
when I am low
I write.
When I am at my highest
I write.
When I can't talk about it,
I simply write it.
I write because
it heals me.

Everyone says,
"Time heals".
But in no form does it truly heal.
Instead, it gives you the strength
to deal with the pain.
Or perhaps,
with each passing day,
we simply get used to living with the pain,
so, it no longer affects us
or rather,
we no longer let it affect us.

I shed my pain like autumn leaves
and made way for springs.
New Beginnings.

We all have our parts to play
in each other's stories.
Everyone has a role in
one another's life…
some teach us how to be,
while others show us how not to be.

Don't let the past deter you
from moving toward the future.

It's okay to hurt.
Experiencing pain is
merely another indication that
you are growing.
One day,
this suffering will come to an end,
and you will emerge from it
a stronger person than before.

Being in pain
and fighting through it every single day
gives you the strength to
overcome and come back
even stronger.

Fighting through pain alone
will make you stronger than before
you'll discover a new version of yourself.
Find your strongest version.

Even if you don't make it,
it's alright.
Regardless of the outcome:
winning or losing…
the journey is what matters,
not the destination.

If you focus on your strength,
your shortcomings will start
to fade away.

It's better to cut ties
with toxic people who
are more like enemies than friends.
Not all farewells are miserable,
Sometimes,
a Farewell can be a relief.
It's time to release yourself.

Keep your distance
if you aren't capable of
the art of healing.

It's far better to end
a deteriorating relationship than
to keep trying to make it work or
to hold out hope that things will
eventually get better.

Although it is painful
to create distance,
it is preferable to
a relationship becoming even more
miserable and the emotional wounds
getting deeper.
Time and space may eventually make
the differences disappear,
and if you happen to cross paths again,
you might end up back together.

Every story must have an inevitable ending.
While some will follow you,
others will move ahead of you.
There will be moments when
you long for the times
and people you have lost.
These collections will be an excellent means
to bring those memories back to life.

Avoid becoming miserable
by trying to fit into the moulds
that society has set.
In a world full of boundless beauty
and opportunity,
follow your passion
as an artist or explorer.

No one gives up on their love;
the door is never truly closed by anyone.
Humans are love creatures.
However,
when that same love gives you
chills or makes you shiver,
you learn to set boundaries,
make decisions to stand out,
and resist the need to burn
and wither.

Seasons bring about changes
in all aspects.
Both the worst and the best
are present in each other.
Adaptability is a necessity,
not a choice,
for healing.

Sometimes,
you need to push away
the person you once wanted
to keep close.

Sometimes,
we fall in love with the wrong person
and get hurt.
However,
the wrong person gives us
the most profound lessons in life.
They give us pain to teach us
how to be strong and self-reliant
and to leverage that agony for power.

Learnings and experiences
are a part of life.

I believe
good people give you
the best memories,
while
bad people give you
the best lessons.
Both are parts of your journey.

Even the worst experiences
give you the best learning.

I was bound by my own sorrow,
anguish, and misery.
It took me a long time to realize
that my grief was a seed rather than
a corpse that was buried.
I had to sprout from a seed buried
deep in the ground
if I was going to overcome
the darkness.

Sometimes,
a moment of silence
is exactly what you need.
You were worn out by
all the things going
on in your life.
You faced numerous battles
that no one knew about,
and you experienced a wide range
of emotions during those days.

You were overcome by
the sheer number of realisations,
you barely had time to pause,
take charge of situation,
and look back
since everything happened so quicky.
Looking back allows you to see
what you missed,
who you lost,
what you had,
what you accomplished,
and even what you did
and how you responded to it.
Take a step back and understand
that everything unfolded for a reason-
it was meant to build your strength.
Express gratitude for all
that took place.

Rather than trying to clean up
the previous mess,
there are times when
we have to start over.
Cleaning up the earlier mess
often makes things worse,
harder, and occupies our minds
with unfavourable thoughts.

When working on old endeavours
begins to bring you down,
you should realize
it's time to let go.

Start something new
something that brings you hope and positivity,
something fresh that renews your enthusiasm,
something that infuses your ideas
with optimism,
and something that offers you
a fresh perspective.

Not everything can be solved
by simply working on it,
there are moments when
you have to start over and
clean up a little.